HAL•LEONARD BASS PLAY•ALONG

JIMI HENDRIX EXPERIENCE SMASH HITS

VOL.

MW00824879

Tracking, mixing, and mastering
by Jake Johnson & Bill Maynard at Paradyme Productions
Bass by Tom McGirr
Guitars by Doug Boduch
Keyboards by Warren Wiegratz
Drums by Scott Schroedl

EXPERIENCE HENDRIX

ISBN-13: 978-1-4234-1420-9
ISBN-10: 1-4234-1420-9

EXCLUSIVELY DISTRIBUTED BY

HAL•LEONARD® CORPORATION

7777 W. BLUEMOUND RD. P.O. BOX 13819 MILWAUKEE, WI 53213

VOL. 10

JIMI HENDRIX EXPERIENCE
SMASH HITS

CONTENTS

Page	Title	Demo Track	Play-Along Track
4	Purple Haze	1	2
10	Fire	3	4
18	The Wind Cries Mary	5	6
23	Can You See Me?	7	8
30	Hey Joe	9	10
38	All Along the Watchtower	11	12
47	Stone Free	13	14
57	Crosstown Traffic	15	16
66	Manic Depression	17	18
75	Remember	19	20
82	Red House	21	22
89	Foxey Lady	23	24
	TUNING NOTES	25	
95	BASS NOTATION LEGEND		

Purple Haze

Words and Music by Jimi Hendrix

Intro

Moderate Rock ♩ = 106

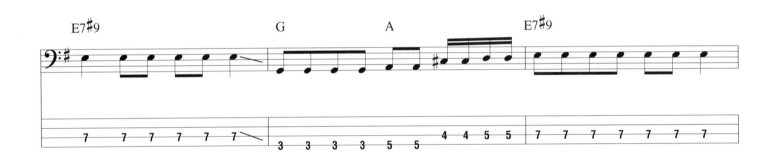

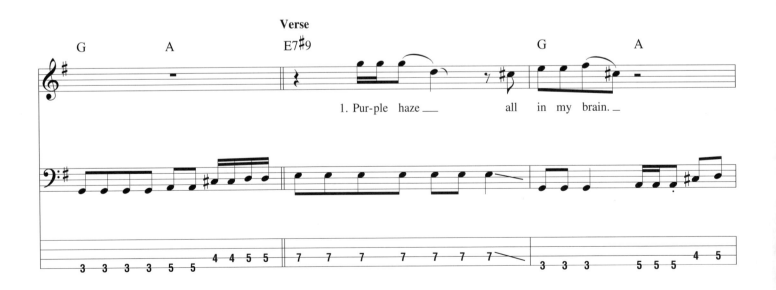

1. Pur-ple haze ___ all in my brain. ___

in mis-er-y? What-ev-er it is, ___ that girl put a spell on me. ___

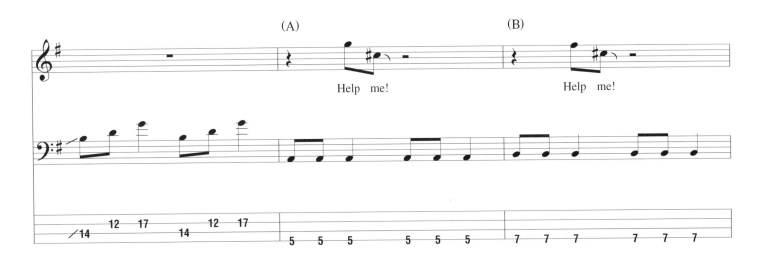

Help me! Help me!

Guitar Solo

Oh, ___ no, ___ no!

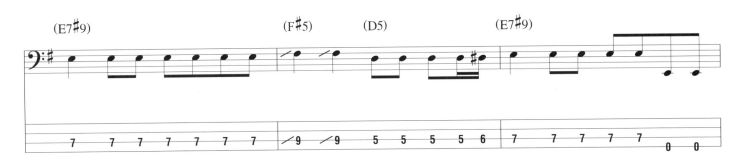

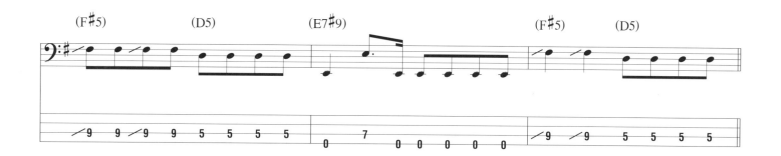

Interlude

N.C.(E5)

Ooh!   Ah!   Ooh!   Ah!

Ooh!   Ah!   Ooh!   Ah!   Yeah!

Verse

E7#9   G   A

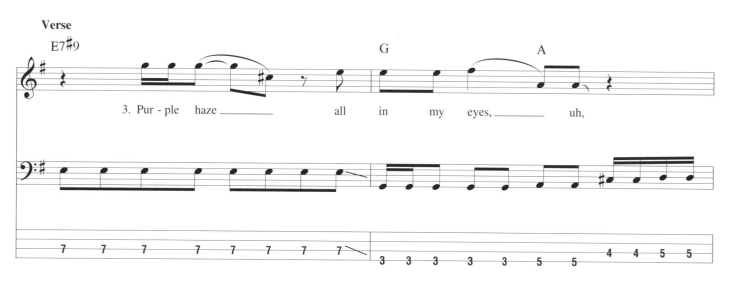

3. Pur - ple haze _____ all in my eyes, _____ uh,

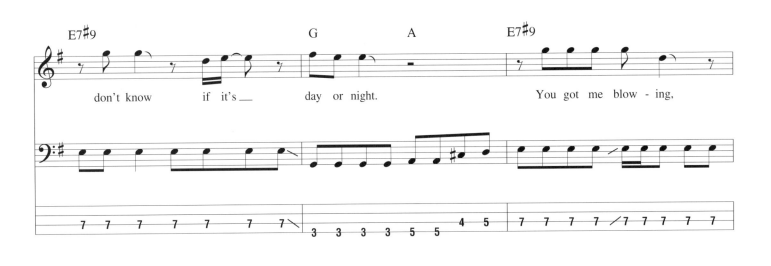

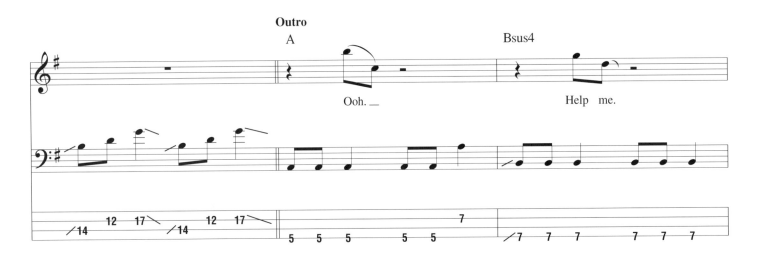

Fire

Words and Music by Jimi Hendrix

Intro
Moderately fast Rock ♩ = 150

Al - right! __

Now dig this, ba - by!

1. You don't care for me, I don't, a, care a - bout __ that. You
2. *See additional lyrics*

got a new fool, __ ha, I like it like __ that. I have __ on - ly one, a,

and stop act-in' so cra-zy. 2. You say your

Coda

Chorus

(Let me stand next to your fire!) Mss - sta! Yeah! Let me stand,

Let me stand next to your fire! ba - by! Let me stand! Let me stand next to your

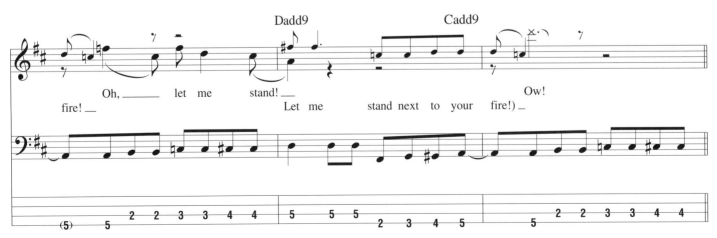

fire! Oh, let me stand! Let me stand next to your fire!) Ow!

Bridge

Oh!__ Move o - ver,__ Rov - er,__ and let Jim - i take

o - ver! Yeah, you know what I'm talk-in' a - bout!

Guitar Solo

Yeah!__ Get on with it, ba - by!

Interlude

N.C.

Spoken: That's what I'm talkin' a - bout. _

(D)

Now, dig this!   Ha!

Verse

N.C.(D)

Now lis - ten, ba - by!   3. You try to   give me your mon-ey,   you bet - ter

save it, babe,   save it for ___ your ___ rain - y day. ___

I have on - ly one, a, burn-in' de - sire, _____ let me stand_ next to your

Chorus

Dadd9   Cadd9

fire, _____ ha!   Ow!   Uh, let me   stand! _

(Let me stand_ next to your fire! ___

Dadd9   Cadd9   Dadd9   Cadd9

___   Oh,   let me   stand,_ ba - by!

Let me   stand_ next to your fire! ___   Let me   stand_ next to your

Ah, __ yes, this is Jim - i talk - in' to you!

(D)

Yeah, __ ba - by!

(E)

Fade out

Do, do, do, do, do, do!

Additional Lyrics

2. You say your mum ain't home, it ain't my concern.
Just, a, play with me and you won't get burned.
I have only one, a, itchin' desire,
Let me stand next to your fire!

The Wind Cries Mary

Words and Music by Jimi Hendrix

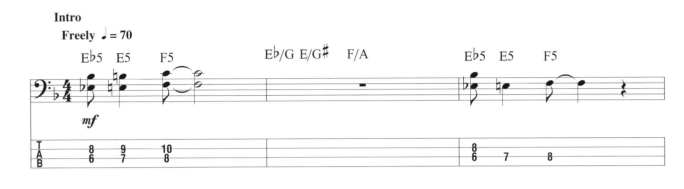

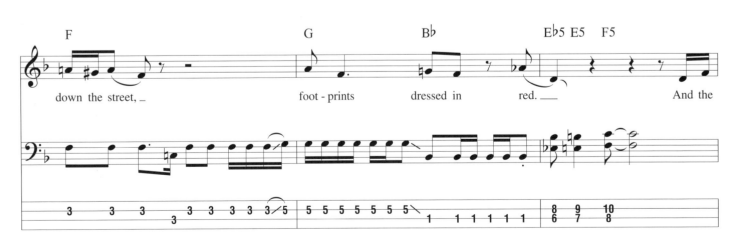

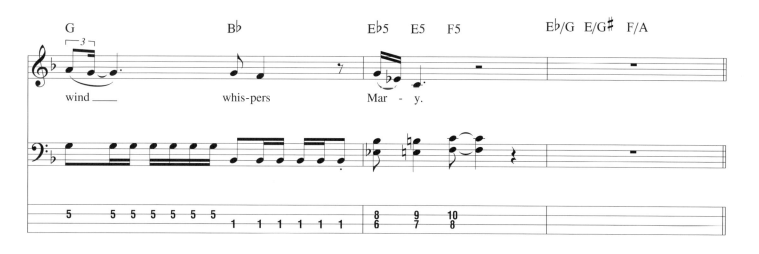

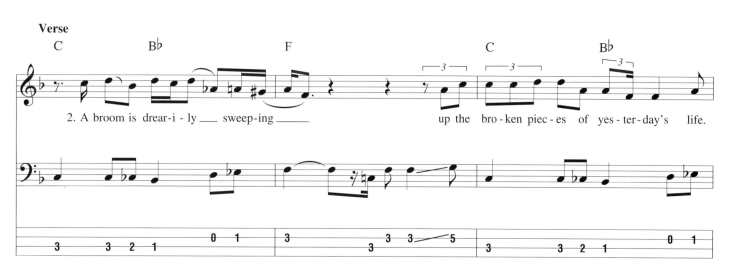

Verse

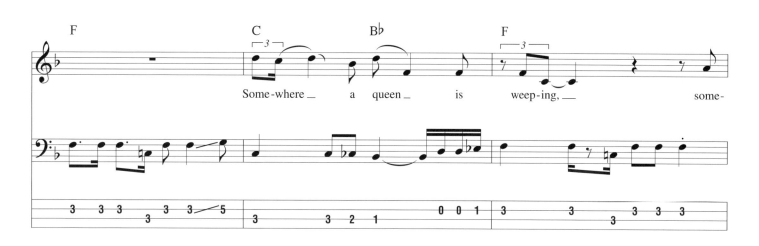

shine their emp-ti-ness down _ on my bed. _ The ti-ny is-land _ sags down-

- stream _ 'cos the life that lived _ is, is dead. _ And the

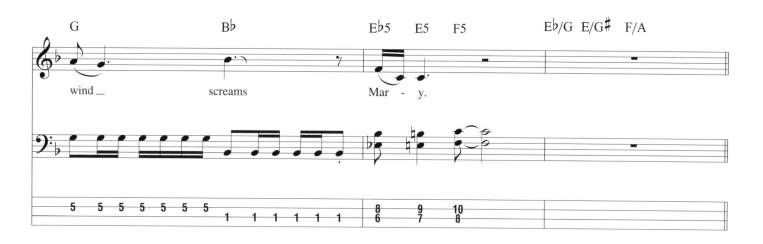

wind _ screams Mar - y.

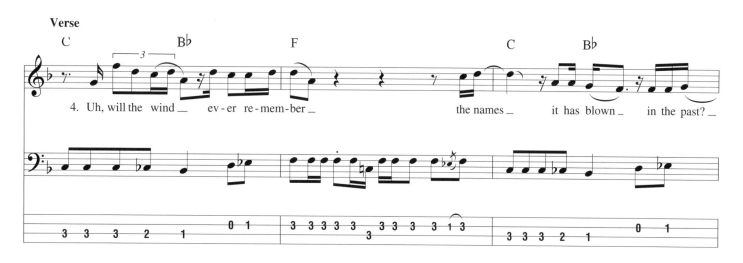

Verse

4. Uh, will the wind _ ev-er re-mem-ber _ the names _ it has blown _ in the past? _

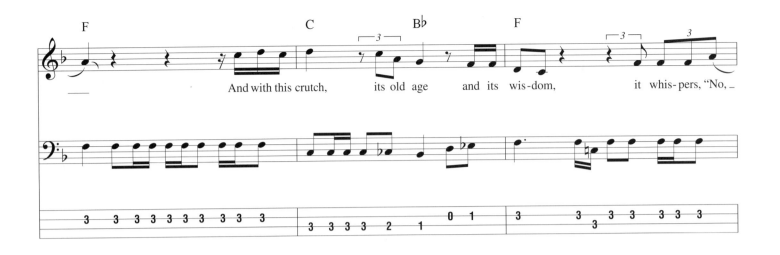

And with this crutch, its old age and its wis-dom, it whis-pers, "No, __

__ this will be the last." __ And the wind __ cries

Mar - y

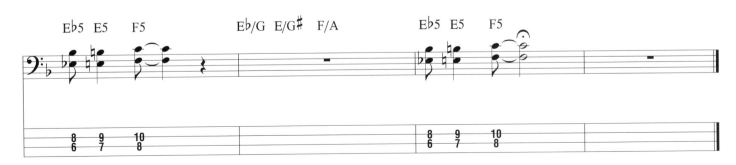

Can You See Me?

Words and Music by Jimi Hendrix

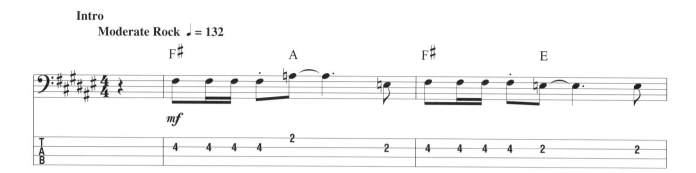

Intro
Moderate Rock ♩ = 132

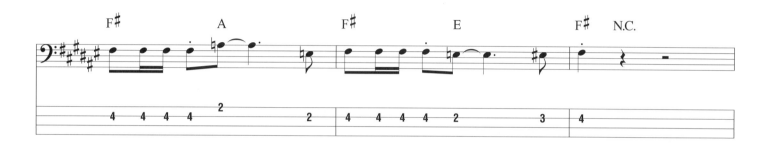

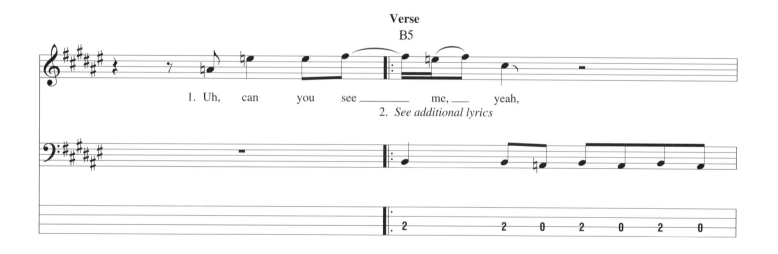

1. Uh, can you see ___ me, ___ yeah,

2. *See additional lyrics*

beg - ging you ___ on my knee?

Whoa, yeah! ___   Can you see ___

___ me, ba - by,   beg - ging please ___ don't   leave? ___

___   Al - right?

If you can see me do - ing that, you can   see in the fu - ture of a

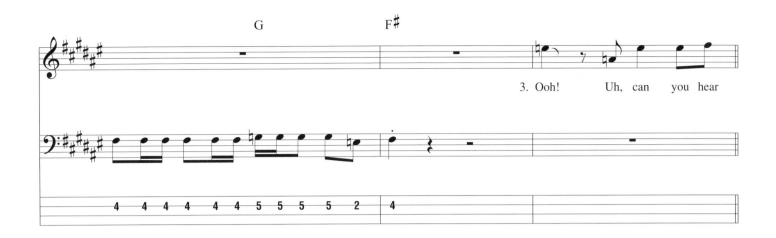

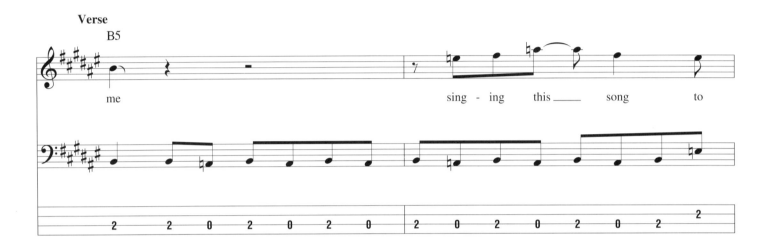

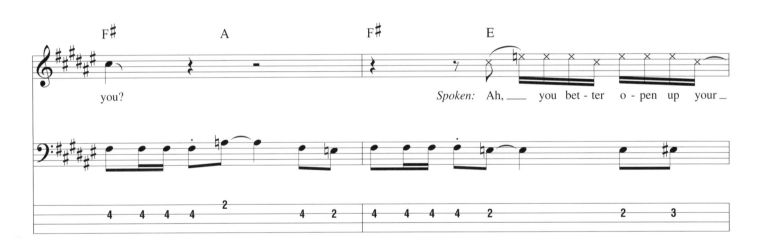

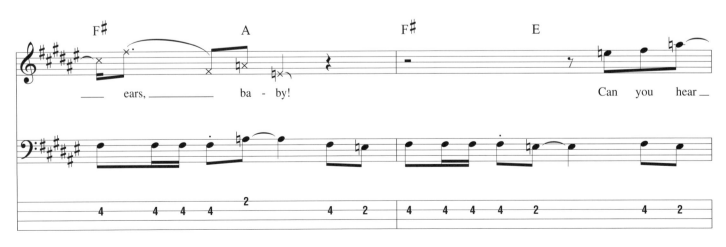

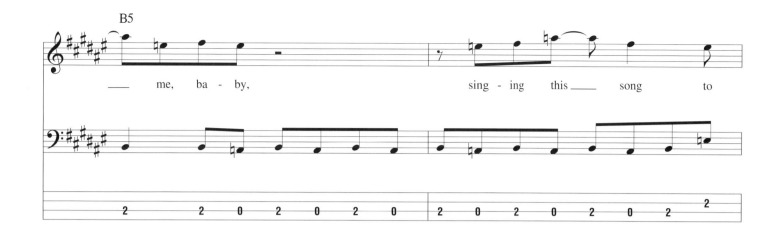

me, ba - by, sing - ing this ___ song to

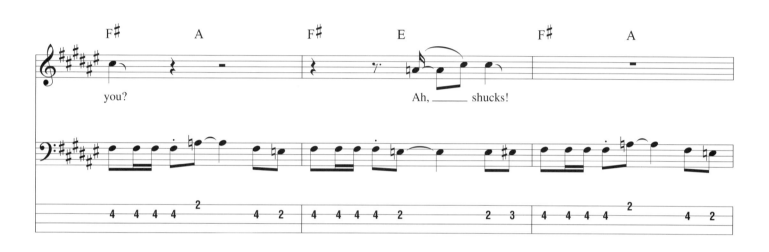

you? Ah, ___ shucks!

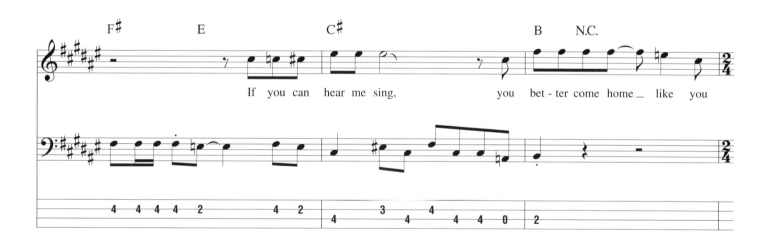

If you can hear me sing, you bet - ter come home ___ like you

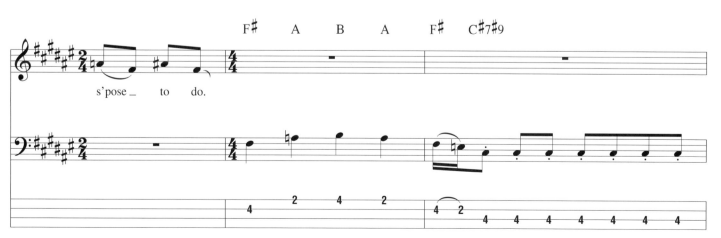

s'pose ___ to do.

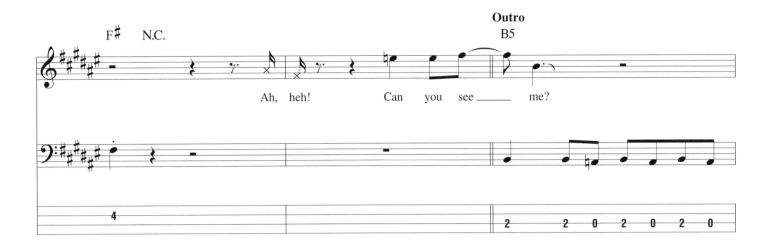

Can you hear _____ me, ba - by?

I don't be - lieve you can. _____

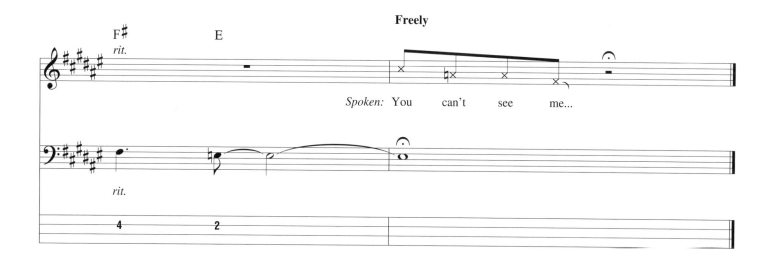

Freely

Spoken: You can't see me...

rit.

Additional Lyrics

2. Uh, can you hear me, yeah, cryin' all over town?
   Yeah, baby.
   Can you hear me, baby, cryin' cos' you put me down?
   Let's reach up, girl.
   If you can hear me doing that, you can
   Hear a freight train coming from a thousand miles.

Hey Joe

Words and Music by Billy Roberts

All Along the Watchtower

Words and Music by Bob Dylan

Tune down 1/2 step:
(low to high) E♭-A♭-D♭-G♭

Intro

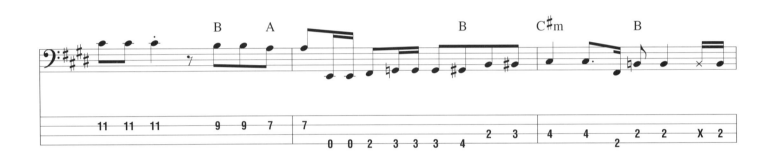

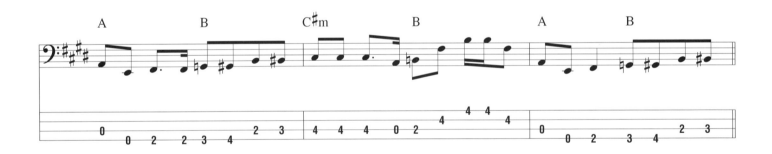

Verse

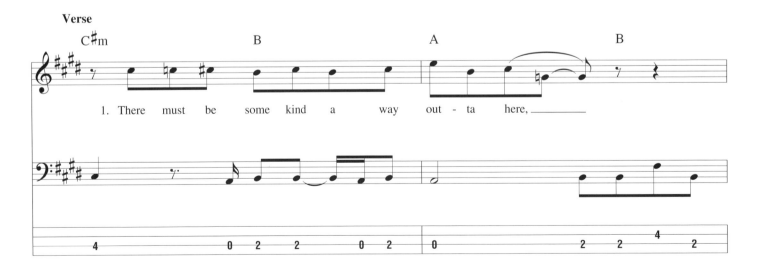

1. There must be some kind a way out-ta here, ___

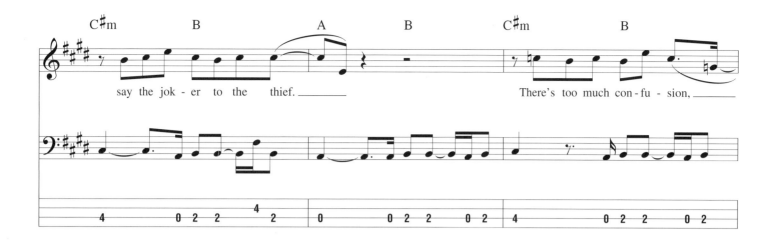

say the jok - er to the thief.____ There's too much con-fu - sion,____

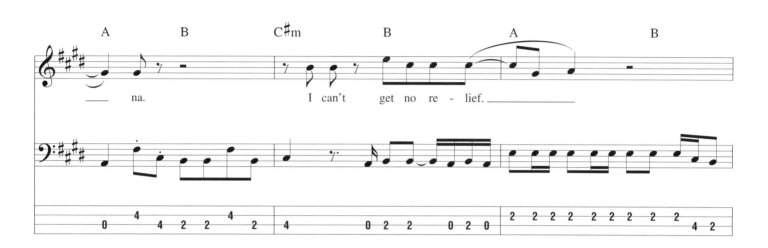

____ na. I can't get no re - lief.____

Busi-ness men, they ah, ah, drink my wine.____ Plow man, dig my earth,____

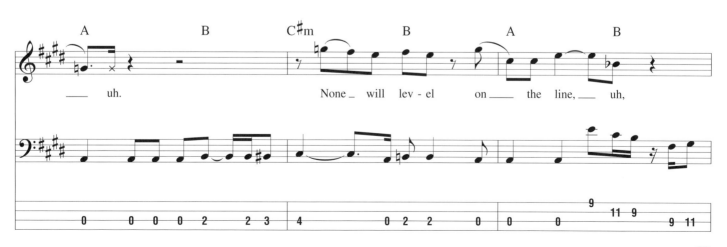

____ uh. None _ will lev - el on ___ the line, ___ uh,

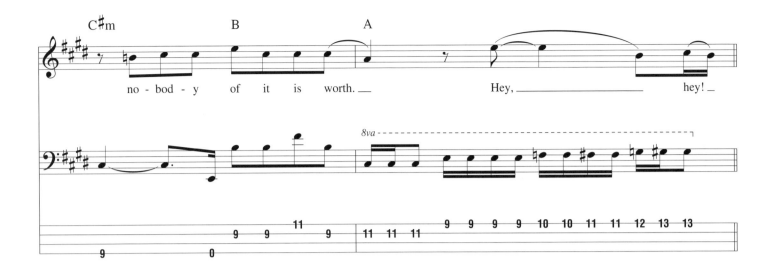

no - bod - y   of   it   is   worth. ___   Hey, _____   hey!

Guitar Solo

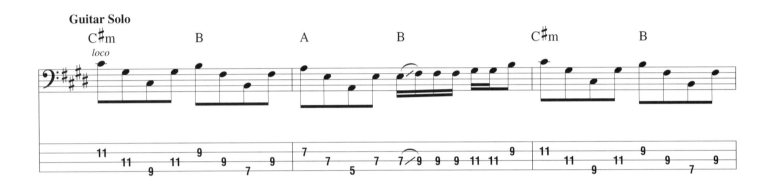

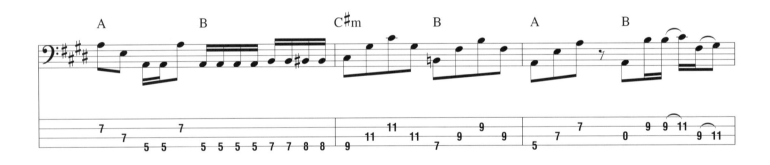

Verse

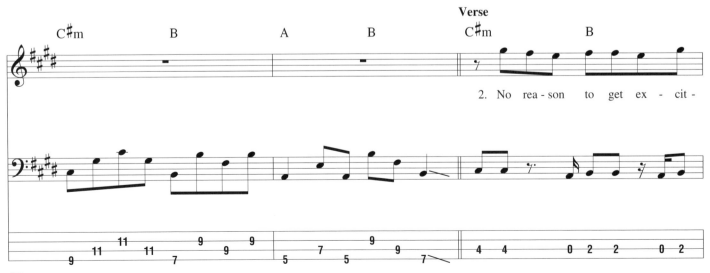

2. No rea - son to get ex - cit -

- ly now, the ho - ur's get - tin' ___ late, ___ ah. Hey! _____

Guitar Solo

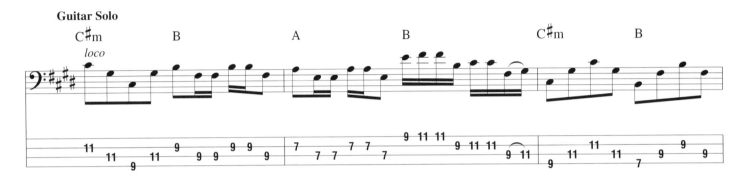

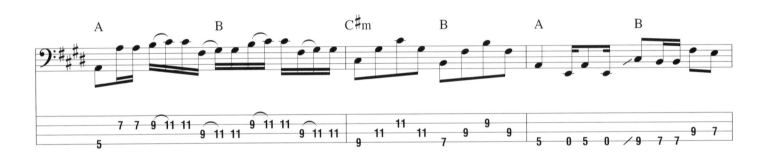

Interlude

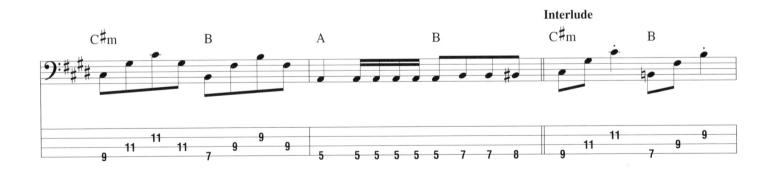

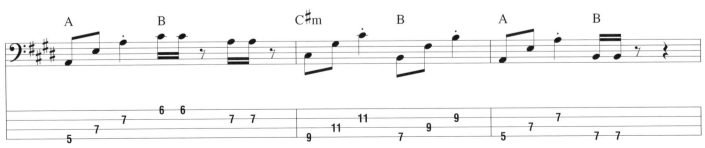

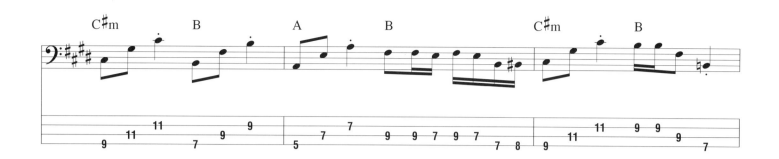

Guitar Solo

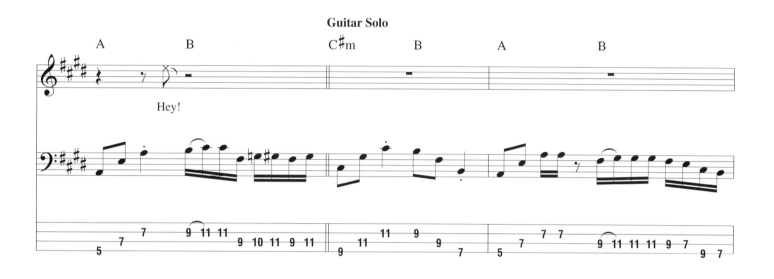

Hey!

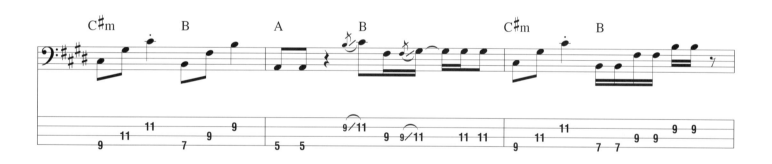

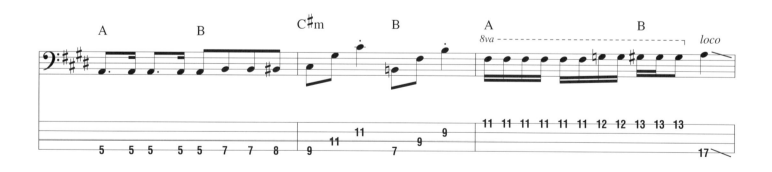

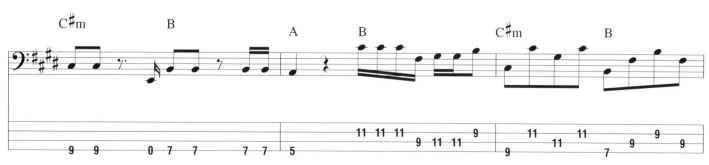

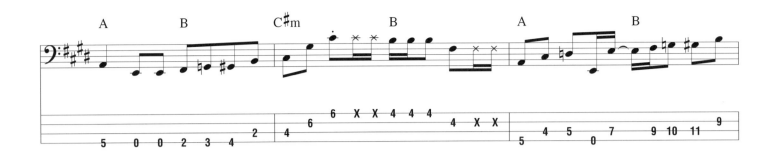

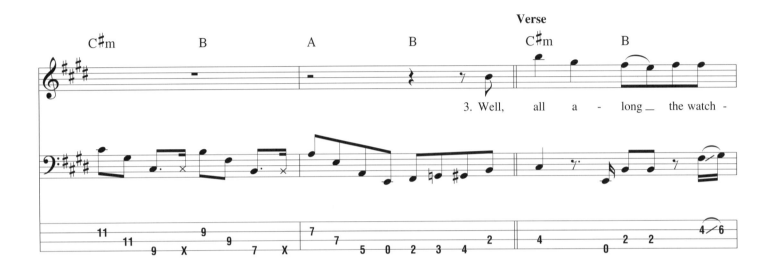

3. Well, all a - long __ the watch -

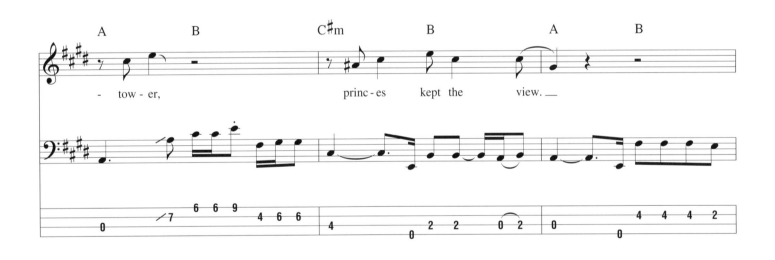

- tow - er,   princ - es   kept the   view. __

While all the wom - en   came __ and went,   bare feet ser - vants   too. __

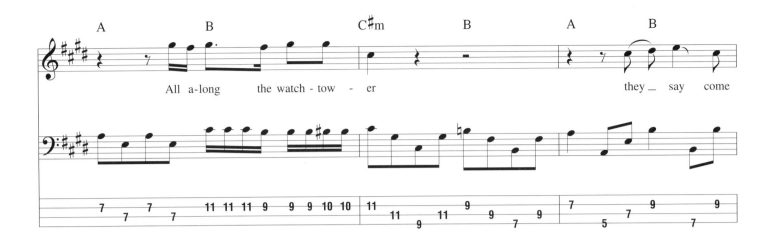

All a-long the watch-tow - er they _ say come

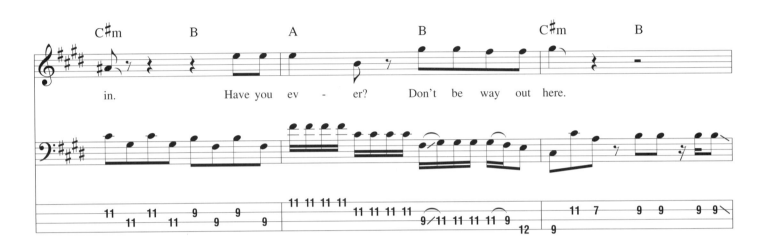

in. Have you ev - er? Don't be way out here.

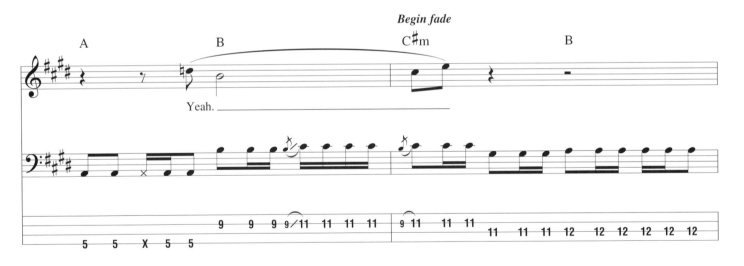

Begin fade

Yeah. _____

Fade out

Ah, babe.

Stone Free

Words and Music by Jimi Hendrix

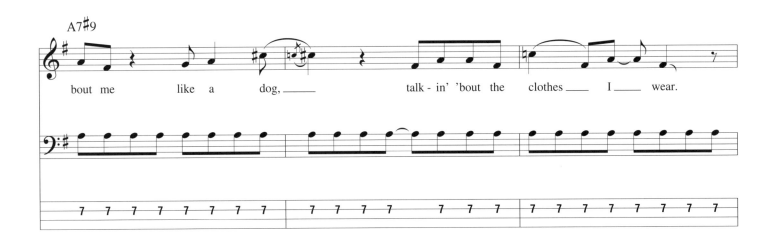

bout me   like a   dog,_____   talk - in' 'bout the   clothes ____ I ____ wear.

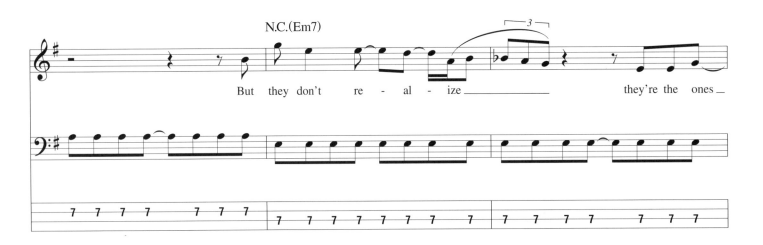

But   they   don't   re - al - ize _____   they're the   ones __

____ who's   square. ____   Hey!   That's why _____

you ___ can't ___ hold ____ me down.   I ____ don't wan -

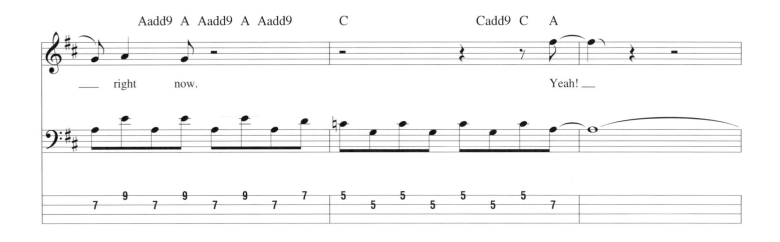

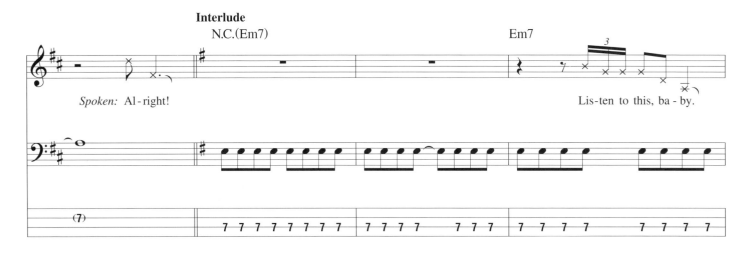

it's so ___ eas-y to break. Oh, but

some-times I get, uh, hot! __ I could feel my heart __ kind-a ___ run-nin' hot. __

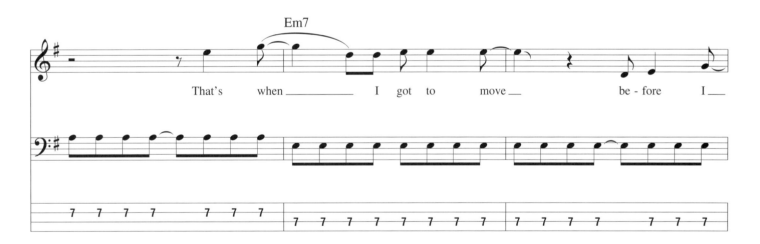

That's when _____ I got to move __ be-fore I __

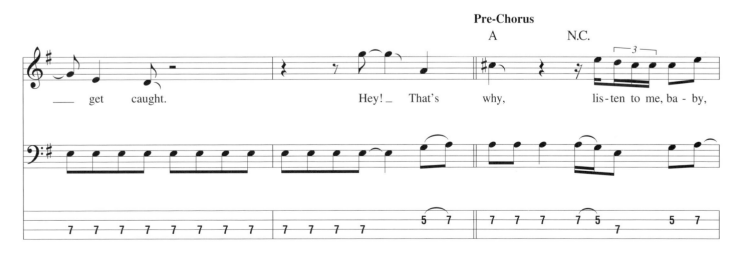

__ get caught. Hey! __ That's why, lis-ten to me, ba-by,

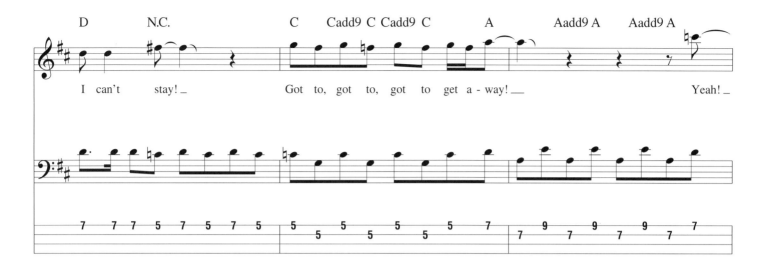

I can't stay! ___ Got to, got to, got to get a-way! ___ Yeah! ___

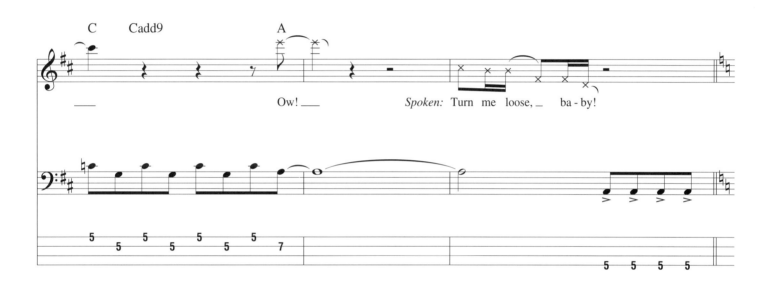

___ Ow! ___ *Spoken:* Turn me loose, ___ ba - by!

Guitar Solo

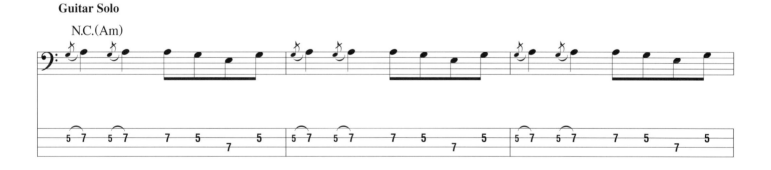

54

Crosstown Traffic

Words and Music by Jimi Hendrix

Tune down 1/2 step:
(low to high) E♭-A♭-D♭-G♭

Intro

Moderately ♩ = 116

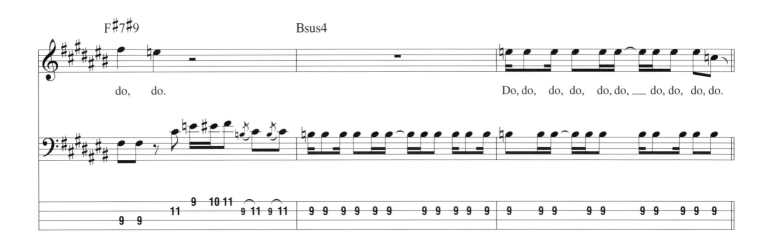

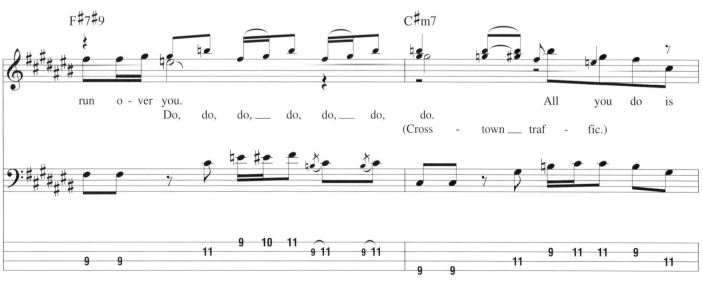

slow me down,
Do, do, do, _____ do, do, do. and I'm try-in' to get on the oth-er side of

Verse

town.
Do, do, do, do, do, do, ___ do, do, do, do.) 2. I'm not the on-ly soul ___ who's

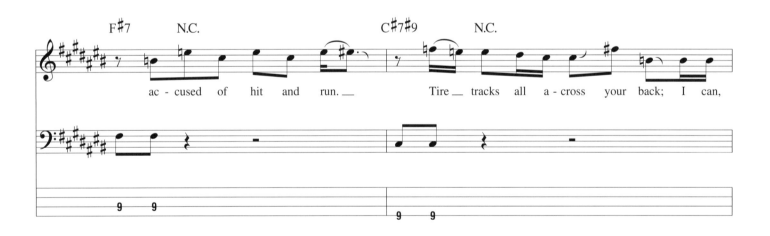

ac - cused of hit and run. ___ Tire ___ tracks all a-cross your back; I can,

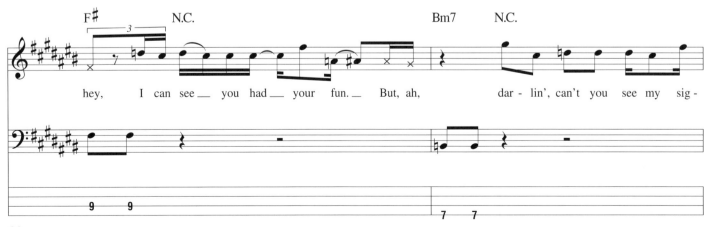

hey, I can see ___ you had ___ your fun. ___ But, ah, dar - lin', can't you see my sig-

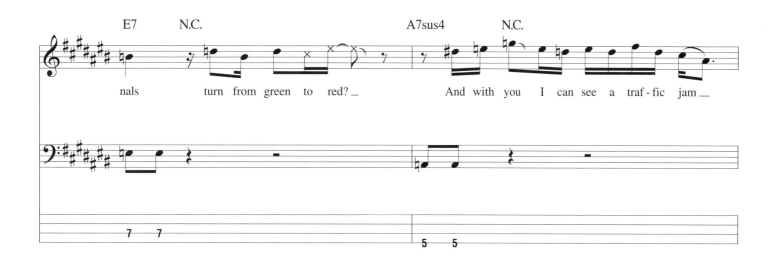

I don't need to run o - ver you.

Cross - town traf - fic. Do, do, do, do, do, do.

All you do is slow me down, an' I

Cross - town traf - fic. Do, do, doo - dle, do, do, do.

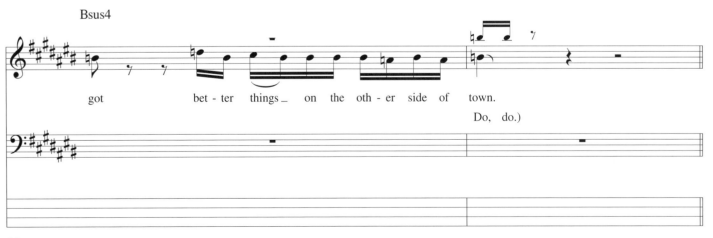

got bet - ter things on the oth - er side of town.

Do, do.)

Guitar Solo

G#7

(Do, do, ___ do, do, do, do, do, do, do, ___ do.

Eadd9

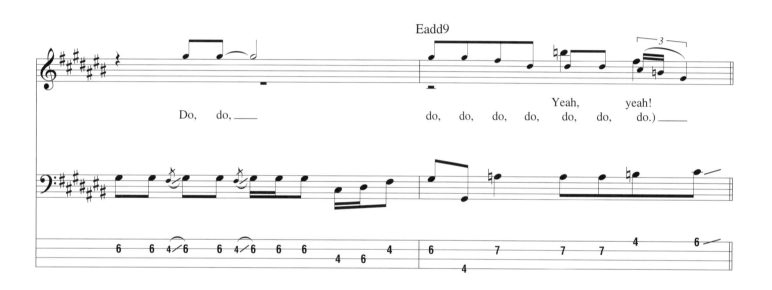

Do, do, ___ Yeah, yeah!
do, do, do, do, do, do, do.) ___

Chorus

C#m7

F#7#9

Look out! Look out.)

(Cross - town traf - fic.
(Do, ___ do, doo - dle, ___ do, do, ___ do, yeah. ___

Look out, ba - by, com - in' through.

Do, do, do, do, do, do,___ do, do, do, do, do, do, do, do,___ do, do, do, do, do, do, do.

C#m7

(Cross - town ___ traf - fic.)

F#7#9

Yeah!

Do, do, do, do, do, do, yeah.___ Look out.

Bsus4

Do, do, do, do, do, do, do, do, do.

C#m7

(Cross - town traf - fic.

Do, do, do, doo - dle, ___ do, do, do,

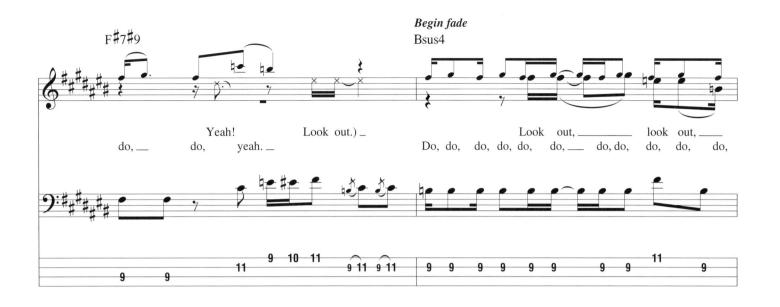

Manic Depression

Words and Music by Jimi Hendrix

Tune down 1/2 step:
(low to high) Eb-Ab-Db-Gb

Intro

Moderate Rock ♩ = 148

*Key signature denotes A Mixolydian.

Verse

1. Man - ic de - pres - sion's _____ touch - ing my soul. _____

I _____ know what I want but I, I

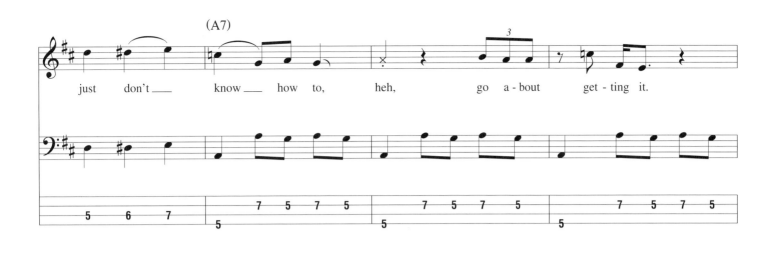

just don't ___ know ___ how to, heh, go a-bout get-ting it.

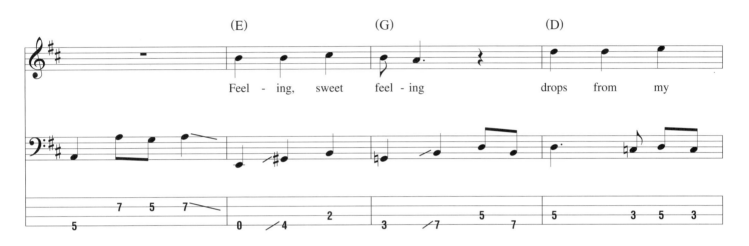

Feel - ing, sweet feel - ing drops from my

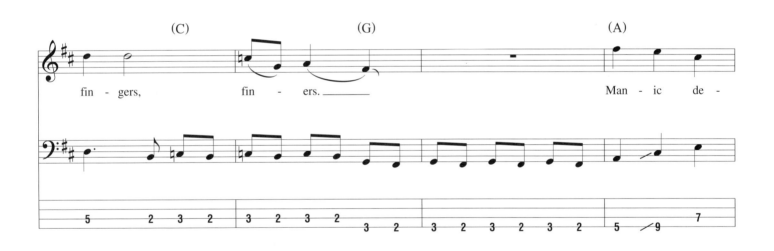

fin - gers, fin - ers. ___ Man - ic de -

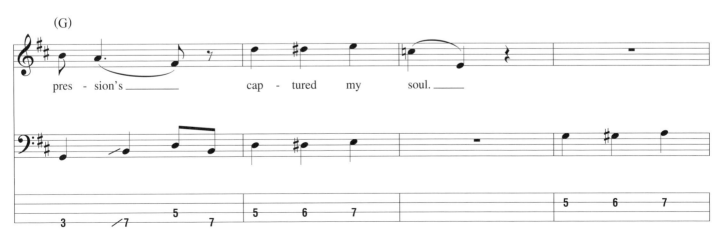

pres - sion's ___ cap - tured my soul. ___

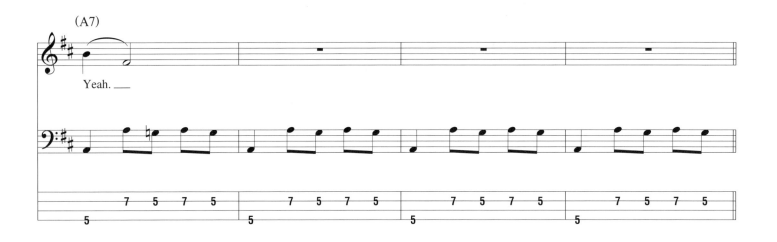

Yeah.

Verse

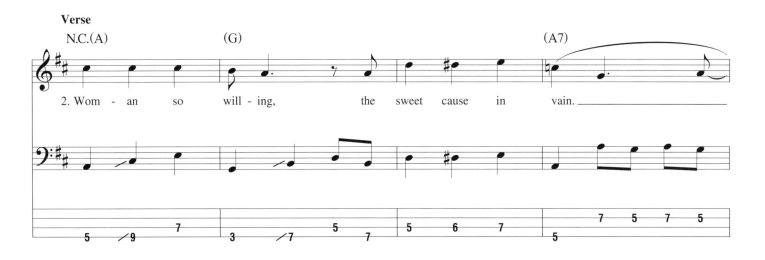

2. Wom-an so will-ing, the sweet cause in vain.

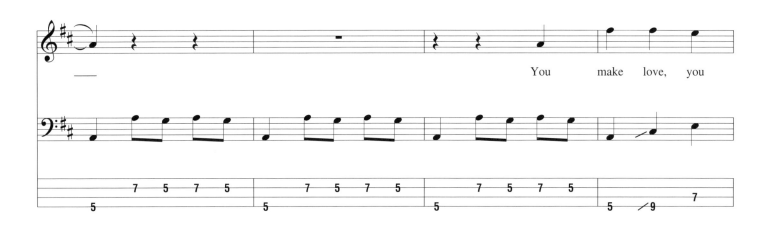

You make love, you

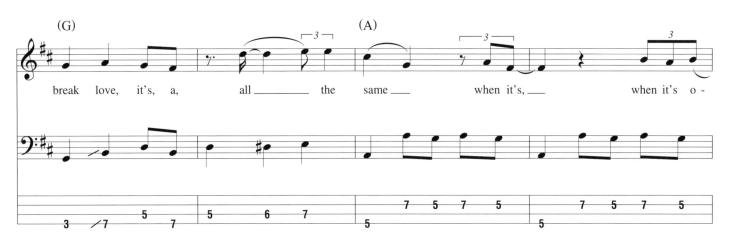

break love, it's, a, all the same when it's, when it's o-

Interlude

Do, _____ do, do, _____

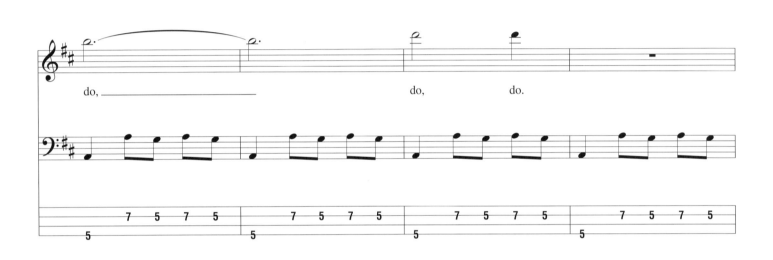

do, _____ do, do.

Guitar Solo

Cry ____ on ____ gui - tar.

Verse

3. Well, I ____ think I'll go turn my-self off ____ and, uh,

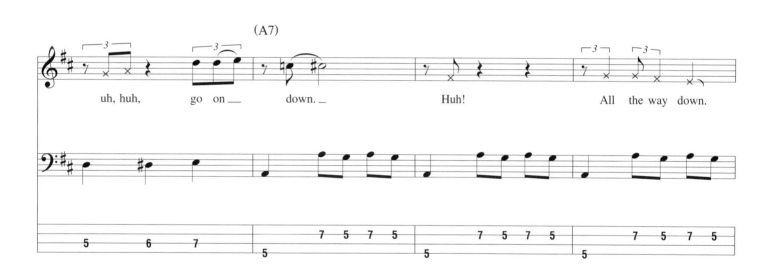

uh, huh, go on ____ down. ____ Huh! All the way down.

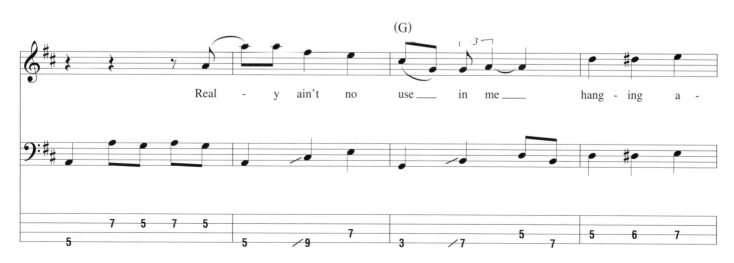

Real - y ain't no use ____ in me ____ hang - ing a -

round ___ in, uh, uh,   your __ kind of scene. _____

Mu - sic, sweet mu - sic,   I wish I could ca - ress _____ and, a,

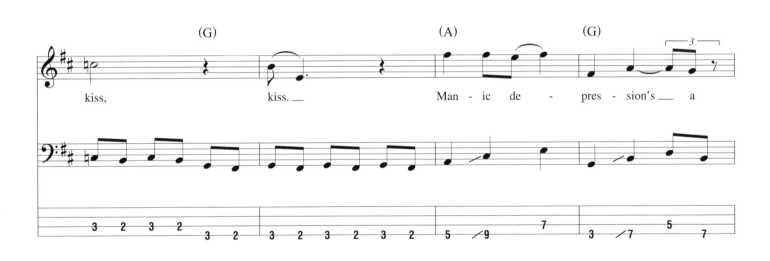

kiss,   kiss. __   Man - ic de - pres - sion's __ a

frus - trat - in' mess!   Oo, ah! _____

Outro

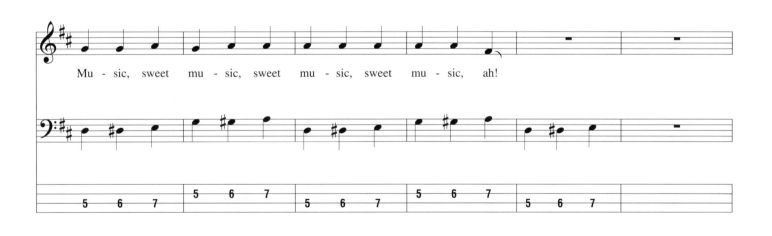

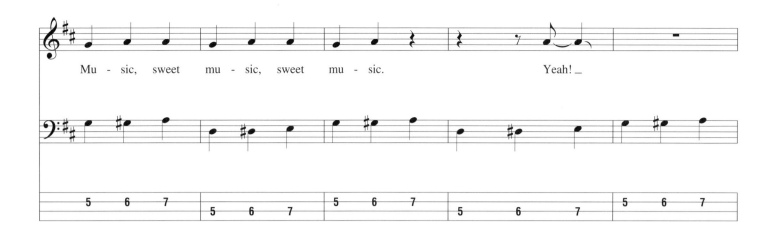

Mu - sic, sweet mu - sic, sweet mu - sic.   Yeah! _

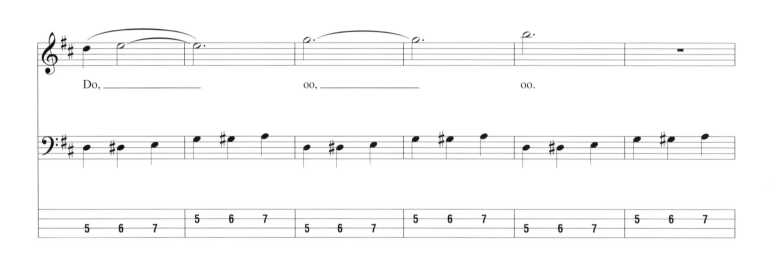

Do, _____ oo, _____ oo.

Fade out

Free time

A5

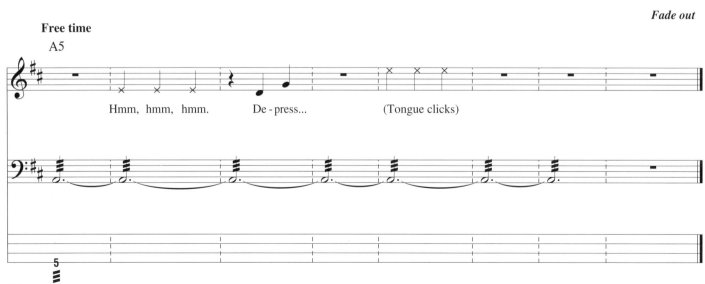

Hmm, hmm, hmm.   De - press...   (Tongue clicks)

74

Remember

Words and Music by Jimi Hendrix

Tune down 1/2 step:
(low to high) Eb-Ab-Db-Gb

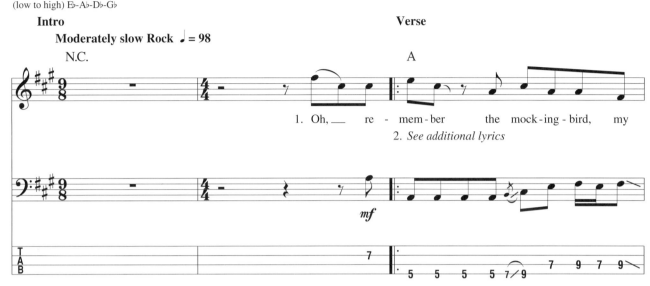

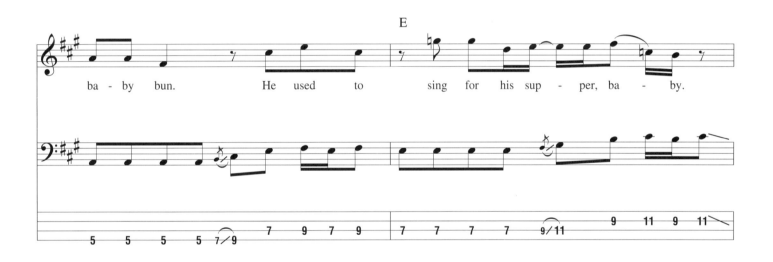

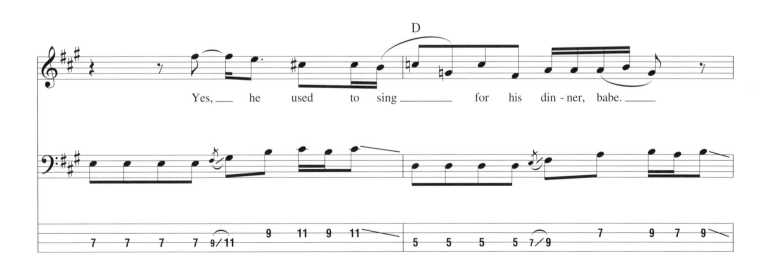

Bridge

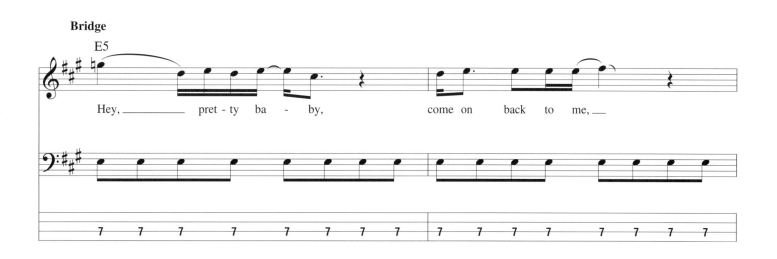

Hey, _____ pret-ty ba - by, come on back to me, ___

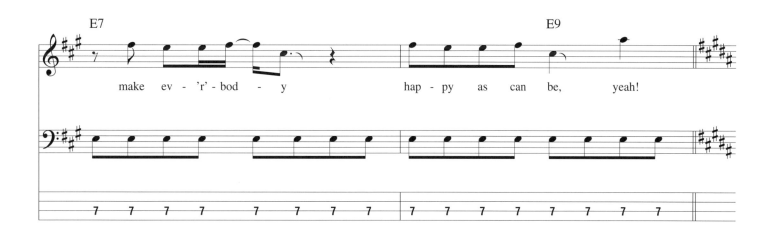

make ev - 'r'- bod - y hap-py as can be, yeah!

Guitar Solo

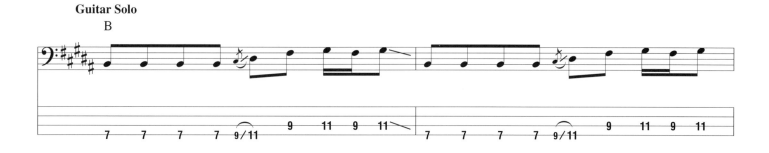

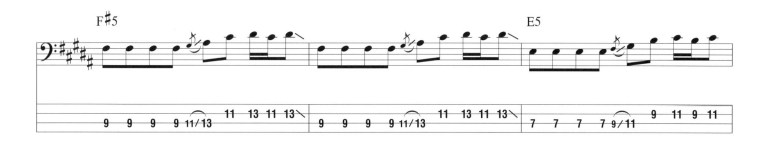

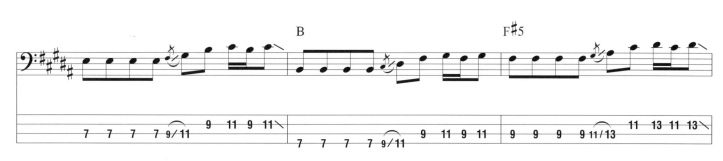

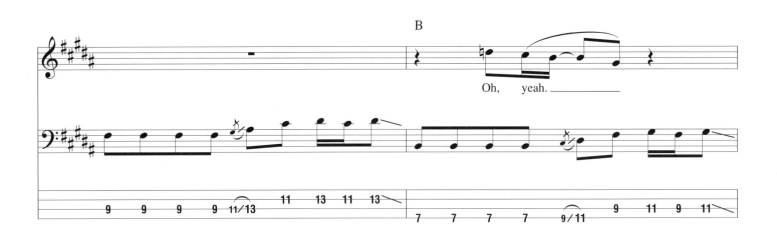

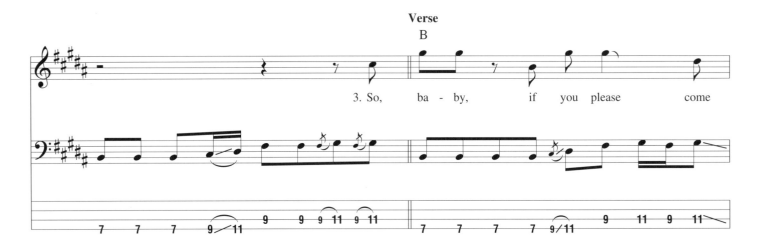

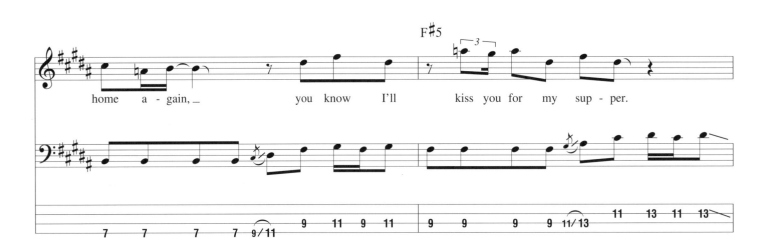

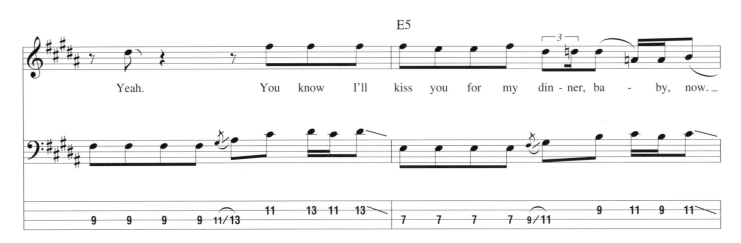

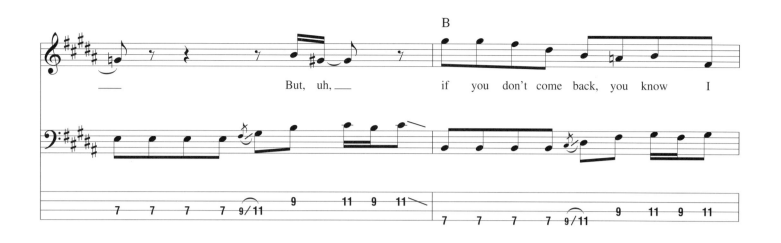

But, uh, ___ if you don't come back, you know I

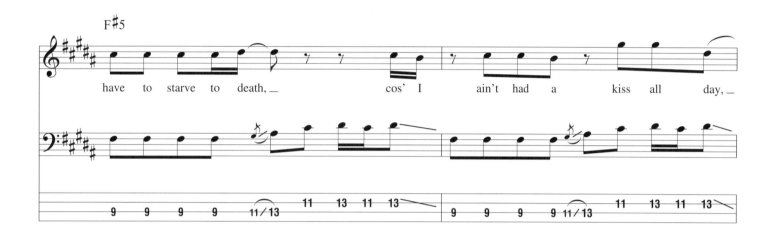

have to starve to death, ___ cos' I ain't had a kiss all day, ___

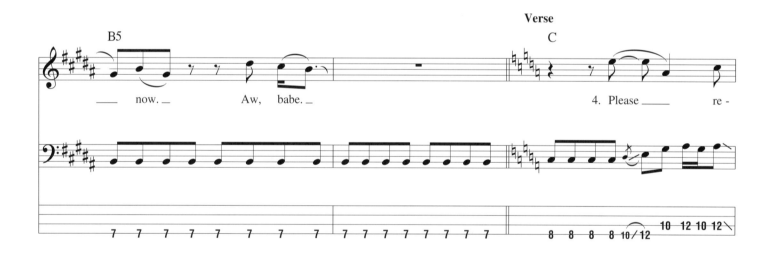

___ now. ___ Aw, babe. ___ 4. Please ___ re -

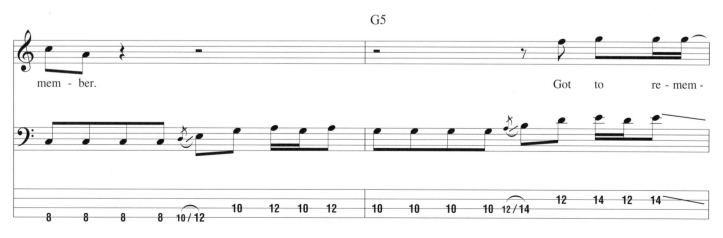

mem - ber. Got to re - mem -

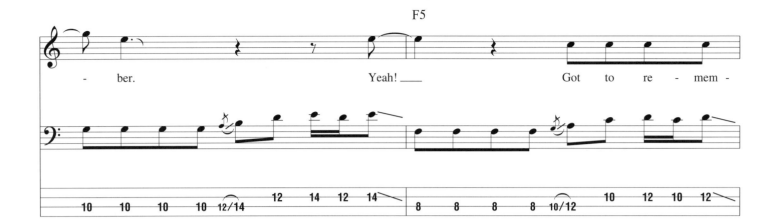

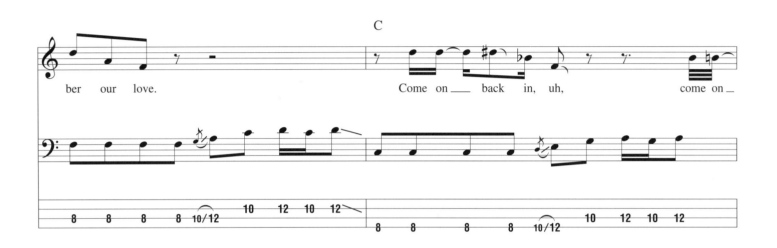

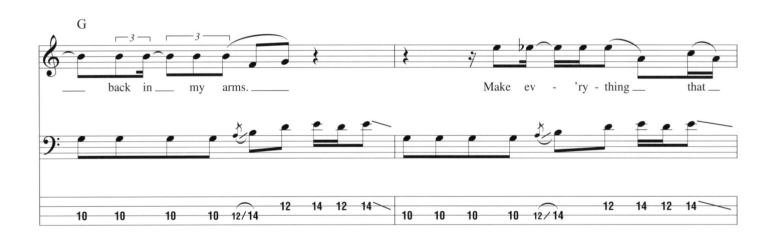

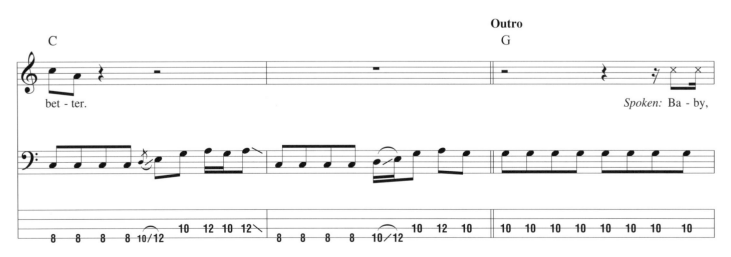

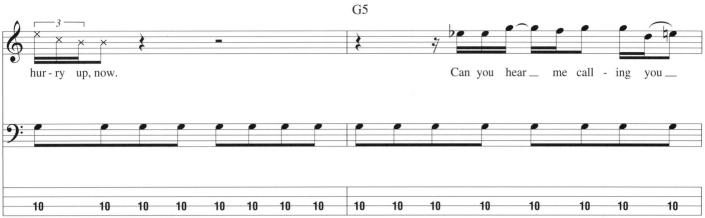

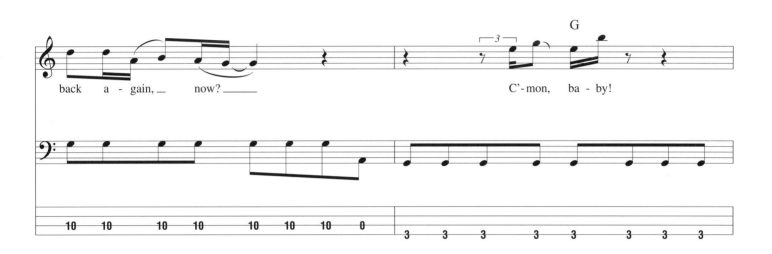

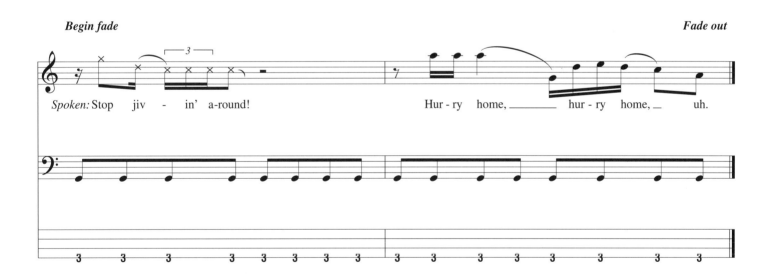

Additional Lyrics

2. Oh, remember the bluebirds and the honey, bees,
   They used to sing for the sunshine.
   Yes, they used to sing for the honey, baby.
   They used to sing so sweet,
   But, a, since my baby left me
   They ain't sang a tune all day. All day.

Red House

Words and Music by Jimi Hendrix

Tune down 1/2 step:
(low to high) E♭-A♭-D♭-G♭

Intro

Moderately slow Blues ♩. = 66

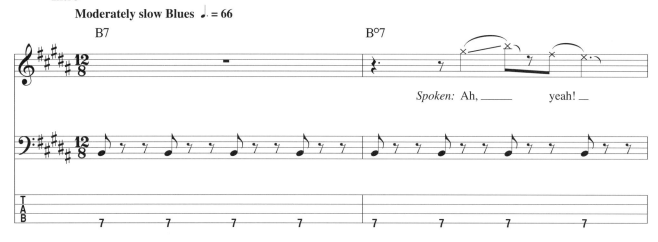

Spoken: Ah, _____ yeah!

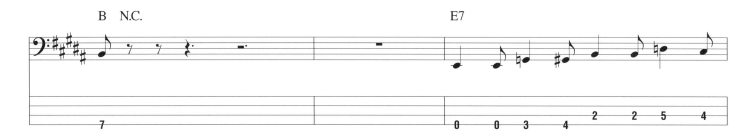

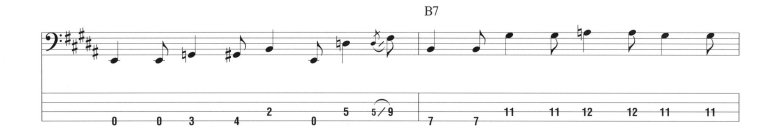

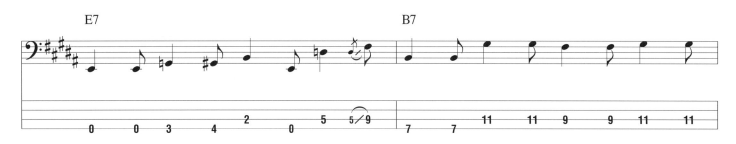

3. Well, I might as well, uh, __

go back o - ver yon - der, __ way back a - mong __ the hills.

Spoken: Yeah, that's what I'm gon - na do. Lord, I

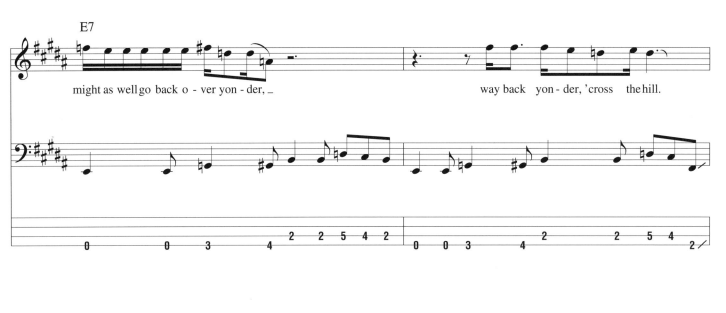

might as well go back o - ver yon - der, _   way back yon - der, 'cross the hill.

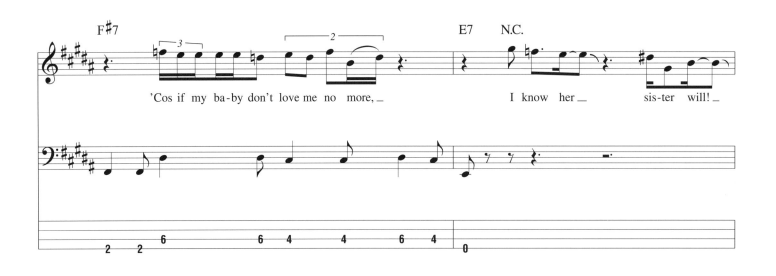

'Cos if my ba-by don't love me no more, _   I know her _ sis-ter will! _

Free time

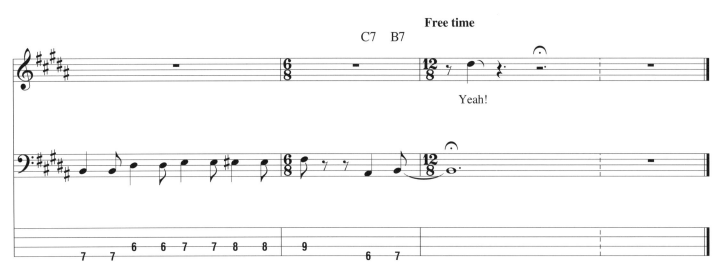

Yeah!

Foxey Lady

Words and Music by Jimi Hendrix

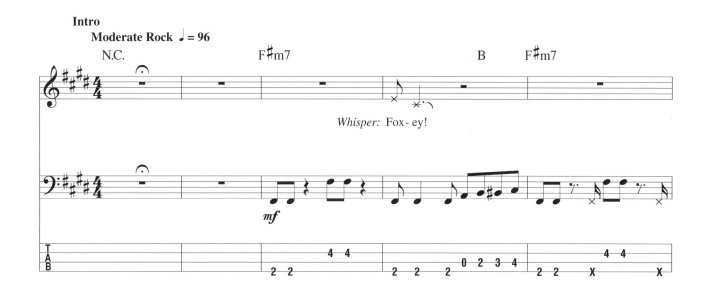

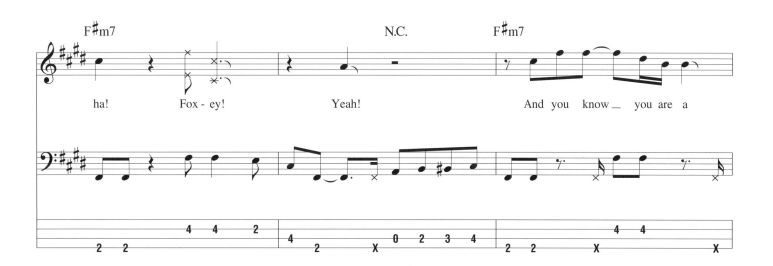

I'm tired___ of wast-ing all my pre-cious time. ___

You got to be all

mine, all mine. ___ Fox-ey__ la-dy! Here I come! __

Guitar Solo

Fox-ey la-dy! Fox-ey la-dy!

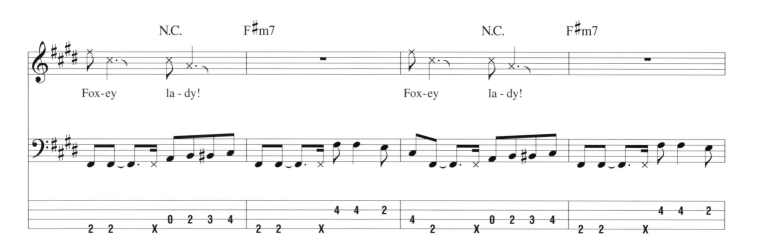

Fox-ey, fox-ey! Fox-ey! Yeah!

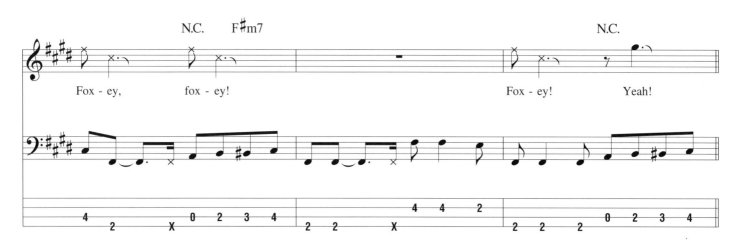

Bass Notation Legend

Bass music can be notated two different ways: on a *musical staff*, and in *tablature*.

THE MUSICAL STAFF shows pitches and rhythms and is divided by bar lines into measures. Pitches are named after the first seven letters of the alphabet.

TABLATURE graphically represents the bass fingerboard. Each horizontal line represents a string, and each number represents a fret.

Notes:

Strings:
high
low

3rd string, open   2nd string, 2nd fret   1st & 2nd strings open, played together

HAMMER-ON: Strike the first (lower) note with one finger, then sound the higher note (on the same string) with another finger by fretting it without picking.

PULL-OFF: Place both fingers on the notes to be sounded. Strike the first note and without picking, pull the finger off to sound the second (lower) note.

LEGATO SLIDE: Strike the first note and then slide the same fret-hand finger up or down to the second note. The second note is not struck.

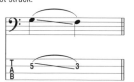

SHIFT SLIDE: Same as legato slide, except the second note is struck.

TRILL: Very rapidly alternate between the notes indicated by continuously hammering on and pulling off.

TREMOLO PICKING: The note is picked as rapidly and continuously as possible.

VIBRATO: The string is vibrated by rapidly bending and releasing the note with the fretting hand.

SHAKE: Using one finger, rapidly alternate between two notes on one string by sliding either a half-step above or below.

NATURAL HARMONIC: Strike the note while the fret hand lightly touches the string directly over the fret indicated.

MUFFLED STRINGS: A percussive sound is produced by laying the fret hand across the string(s) without depressing them and striking them with the pick hand.

BEND: Strike the note and bend up the interval shown.

BEND AND RELEASE: Strike the note and bend up as indicated, then release back to the original note. Only the first note is struck.

RIGHT-HAND TAP: Hammer ("tap") the fret indicated with the "pick-hand" index or middle finger and pull off to the note fretted by the fret hand

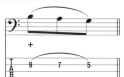

LEFT-HAND TAP: Hammer ("tap") the fret indicated with the "fret-hand" index or middle finger.

SLAP: Strike ("slap") string with right-hand thumb.

POP: Snap ("pop") string with right-hand index or middle finger.

Additional Musical Definitions

   (accent)   • Accentuate note (play it louder).

   (accent)   • Accentuate note with great intensity.

   (staccato)   • Play the note short.

    • Downstroke

V   • Upstroke

D.S. al Coda   • Go back to the sign (𝄋), then play until the measure marked "*To Coda*," then skip to the section labelled "**Coda**."

D.C. al Fine   • Go back to the beginning of the song and play until the measure marked "*Fine*" (end).

Bass Fig.   • Label used to recall a recurring pattern.

Fill   • Label used to identify a brief melodic figure which is to be inserted into the arrangement.

tacet   • Instrument is silent (drops out).

   • Repeat measures between signs.

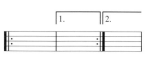   • When a repeated section has different endings, play the first ending only the first time and the second ending only the second time.

NOTE: Tablature numbers in parentheses mean:
1. The note is being sustained over a system (note in standard notation is tied), or
2. The note is sustained, but a new articulation (such as a hammer-on, pull-off, slide or vibrato) begins, or
3. The note is a barely audible "ghost" note (note in standard notation is also in parentheses).

95

HAL·LEONARD BASS PLAY·ALONG

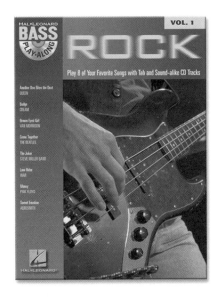

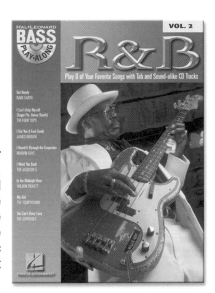

The Bass Play-Along Series will help you play your favorite songs quickly and easily! Just follow the tab, listen to the CD to hear how the bass should sound, and then play along using the separate backing tracks. The melody and lyrics are also included in the book in case you want to sing, or to simply help you follow along. The audio CD is playable on any CD player. For PC and Mac computer users, the CD is enhanced so you can adjust the recording to any tempo without changing pitch!

Rock VOLUME 1
Songs: Another One Bites the Dust • Badge • Brown Eyed Girl • Come Together • The Joker • Low Rider • Money • Sweet Emotion.
00699674 Book/CD Pack $12.95

R&B VOLUME 2
Songs: Get Ready • I Can't Help Myself (Sugar Pie, Honey Bunch) • I Got You (I Feel Good) • I Heard It Through the Grapevine • I Want You Back • In the Midnight Hour • My Girl • You Can't Hurry Love.
00699675 Book/CD Pack $12.95

Pop/Rock VOLUME 3
Songs: Crazy Little Thing Called Love • Crocodile Rock • Maneater • My Life • No Reply at All • Peg • Message in a Bottle • Suffragette City.
00699677 Book/CD Pack $12.95

'90s Rock VOLUME 4
Songs: All I Wanna Do • Fly Away • Give It Away • Hard to Handle • Jeremy • Know Your Enemy • Spiderwebs • You Oughta Know.
00699679 Book/CD Pack $12.95

Funk VOLUME 5
Songs: Brick House • Cissy Strut • Get Off • Get Up (I Feel Like Being) a Sex Machine • Higher Ground • Le Freak • Pick up the Pieces • Super Freak.
00699680 Book/CD Pack $12.95

Classic Rock VOLUME 6
Songs: Free Ride • Funk #49 • Gimme Three Steps • Green-Eyed Lady • Radar Love • Werewolves of London • White Room • Won't Get Fooled Again.
00699678 Book/CD Pack $12.95

Hard Rock VOLUME 7
Songs: Crazy Train • Detroit Rock City • Iron Man • Livin' on a Prayer • Living After Midnight • Peace Sells • Smoke on the Water • The Trooper.
00699676 Book/CD Pack $12.95

Prices, contents and availability subject to change without notice.

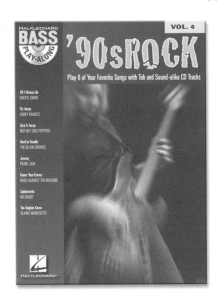

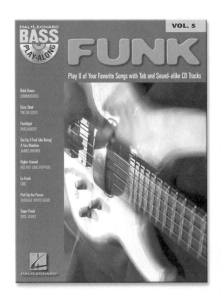

FOR MORE INFORMATION,
SEE YOUR LOCAL MUSIC DEALER,
OR WRITE TO:

HAL·LEONARD®
CORPORATION
7777 W. BLUEMOUND RD. P.O. BOX 13819
MILWAUKEE, WISCONSIN 53213

Visit Hal Leonard Online at **www.halleonard.com**